p

What's in This Book

How do we know that the huge dinosaurs ever existed? After all, no humans were around to see them. And how are scientists able to figure out what Earth looked like during different periods of its vast history? The answers to these questions, and many more, can be found in a trail of natural clues called fossils that Earth's creatures have left behind, usually buried in rocks or beneath the ground. *What Fossils Tell Us: The History of Life* examines the ever-unfolding stories these fossils reveal about life on Earth. Dig in and learn how fossils were formed, and find out about some of the important people and places in the field of paleontology (the study of fossils and ancient life).

The COME LEARN WITH ME series encourages children's natural curiosity about the world by introducing them to exciting areas in science. Each book deals with a specific topic, and can be read alone or together with an adult. With lively, reader-friendly texts and numerous engaging illustrations, the books will entertain and inform children and adults alike. No previous knowledge of the subject is needed. Scientific vocabulary appears in **bold type** and is defined in context, but is also listed in the Glossary at the end of the book. Let these books be your guide as you enter the fascinating world of science, where you are sure to discover many new interests and vastly expand your horizons.

COME LEARN WITH ME

What Fossils Tell Us: The History of Life

Text by Bridget Anderson

BANK STREET COLLEGE OF EDUCATION
in association with the
AMERICAN MUSEUM OF NATURAL HISTORY
for Lickle Publishing Inc

Library of Congress Control Number
2002113574
ISBN: 1-890674-13-3

ILLUSTRATION AND PHOTO CREDITS

American Museum of Natural History: 6-7c, 7l, 8 tr, 8bl, 9t, 9b, 9c, 10-11, 12tr, 14tr, 14-15, 15bl, 16tr, 17t, 17cr, 18cl, 19tl, 22-23b, 23cr, 30tr, 32tl, 35br, 38c, 38br, 39tl, 39tr, 39c, 43t, 44tl, 45cl—AMNH photographers J. Beckett 14bl; J. Beckett/C. Chesek 13t; J. Beckett/K. Perkins 40tr; C. Chesek 18bl, 19br, 36t; Jim Coxe 6l, 8r, 12-13c, 19tr; Denis Finnin, 1t, 2-3, 10t, 14cl, 14bl, 18t, 20tr, 20br, 32-33b, 33tr, 36b, 37t, 37c, 40b, 41t, 41c, 45br J.N. Knull 35t; G. G. Lower 19cl; R. Merkens 21, 27tr; F. H. Pough 17bl, 28l, 29r; B Anderson: 16bl; BP p.l.c. (2002) 44-45c; Badlands National Park: 12bl; Elizabeth Gibbs 26bl, 44b; Stephen Durr 28cr; George C. Page Museum 42b, 43br; Lisa-ann Gershwin 31t, 31cr, 31c; Pamela J. W. Gore, Georgia Perimeter College 19bl; Lickle Stables 22t; Lochman Transparencies: Eva Boogaard 28br; Dr. Anatoly Louzhin, North East Interdisciplinary Scientific Research Institute, Russian Academy of Sciences, Far East Branch, Magadan 15tl; Andrew MacRae 34tl, 34tr, 34bl, 34br; NASA: 7t; National Oceanic and Atmospheric Administration (NOAA) Photo Library 30bl—NOAA photographer, Commander William Harrigan 20bl; Institute of Biological Sciences, Gene Experimental Center, Tskuba University, Japan, courtesy Prof. Tanaka 29cl; USGS 24-25, 26tr, 27bl; Giselle Walker, Natural History Museum, London 31bl;

Illustrations: Chris Forsey 10-11b

Series Director: Charles Davey
Text by Bank Street College of Education:
Andrea Perelman, Project Manager; Elisabeth Jakab, Project Editor
Photographs unless otherwise credited from the American Museum of Natural History:
Maron L. Waxman, Editorial Director; Carl Mehling, Consultant
Art Direction, Production & Design: Charles Davey, Charles Davey design LLC
Photo research: Erin Barnett

Printed in Hong Kong

CONTENTS

Life on Earth

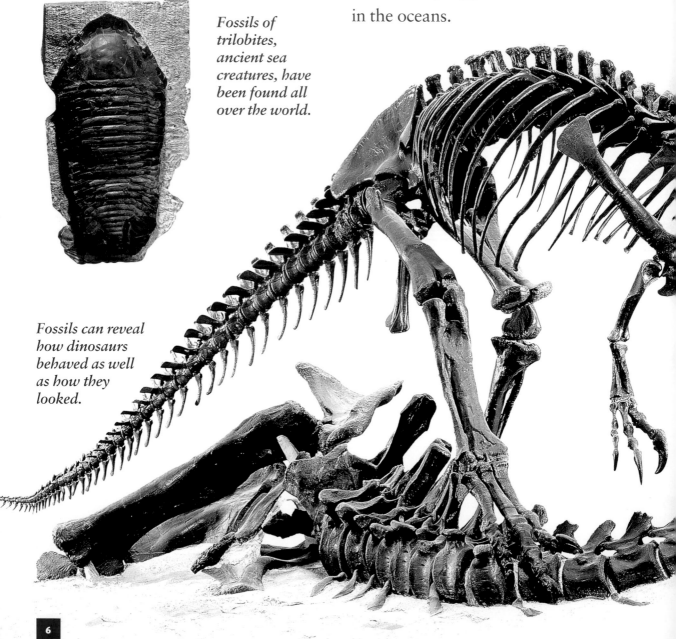

Earth is a beautiful place. It is full of life in thick green forests, dry deserts, snowy mountains, flowing rivers, and deep, vast oceans. But Earth hasn't always looked this way. The plants and animals alive today are only a tiny sample of the hundreds of millions of different organisms that have lived on Earth throughout its history.

Many of Earth's most fascinating creatures have disappeared forever. Small, many-legged trilobites once lived in the oceans.

Fossils of trilobites, ancient sea creatures, have been found all over the world.

Fossils can reveal how dinosaurs behaved as well as how they looked.

Enormous dinosaurs roamed through tropical swamps. Woolly mammoths braved the snow and cold of the ice ages. Earth is extremely old, and life has had a long time to change.

Earth is an ever-changing planet.

Paleontologist Luis Chiappe uncovers an Oviraptor *skeleton in the Gobi Desert, Mongolia.*

Humans, on the other hand, have been around only recently. No people ever saw giant dinosaurs and trilobites living on Earth. So how do we know anything about them? How do we know what Earth looked like long before humans were alive? Luckily, there is a trail of clues that reveals much about life long ago.

These clues are **fossils**.

What Are Fossils?

Fossils are any evidence of ancient organisms (living things) that have been preserved over time. They help scientists piece together the story of Earth's past. When you picture a fossil, you might think of a dinosaur skeleton or the shell of a sea animal. But there are fossils of almost every kind of living thing— plants, insects, mushrooms, even jellyfish.

These fossil backbones show tooth marks, possibly from an ancient battle.

Sometimes, ancient animals left behind marks such as footprints or tooth marks that also became preserved. Scientists have even found ancient dinosaur dung! Scientists call all these things **trace fossils**, because they show traces of an animal even though its body is not found. They also give scientists clues to how an animal behaved and moved when it was alive.

Fossils of leaves, such as Coculus haydenianus, *can be quite beautiful.*

This rock, called coprolite, is actually fossilized dinosaur dung.

The rock surfaces inside caves can be good places to find fossils.

Millions of fossils have been found on every **continent** on Earth. The word "fossil" comes from an old word, *fossilis*, which means "dug-up." That is exactly what people have to do to find most fossils— dig them up out of the ground.

Some fossils have been discovered by accident, but most are found by the careful searching of **paleontologists**, scientists who study ancient life, and other fossil collectors.

Anyone can find a fossil if he or she knows where to search. Look carefully in the rocks along the roadside, in dunes along the beach, and in the walls of buildings made of limestone. Dig in places where people have found fossils before. Wind and rain continually wash away soil and rock exposing new fossils over time.

Paleontologists carefully excavate (uncover) fossils using tools including chisels and paintbrushes.

How Many Fossils Form

This fossil of a sturgeon has been preserved so well that you can see its bones and fins.

Imagine life in an ancient sea. When a fish dies, it usually sinks to the sea floor. Other animals eat away its flesh, leaving just the bones. Sea currents wash sand over the bones, and they quickly become buried. On the land nearby, rivers wash sediment such as mud, silt, and rocks down to the ocean where it settles on the seafloor over the sand. Many more layers of sediment are added over time.

Sediment is heavy. Has anyone ever covered you with sand at the beach? The more sand they put on you, the heavier it feels. Pretty soon it's hard to move. Something similar happens to the sand layer holding the fish. Slowly the sand grains are pressed together until they harden into a **sedimentary rock** called sandstone. The fish remains are trapped inside the rock.

Water slowly seeps through the layers of sedimentary rock and into the sandstone. **Minerals**, chemicals that form rock, are carried by the water and deposited into tiny holes in the fish bones. These minerals change and harden the bones.

Over time, the original bone material can be completely replaced by minerals. If this happens, the fish has turned to stone. This process is called **mineralization**.

Many years later, these layers of sedimentary rock can be exposed if the water level drops or they are pushed up out of the ocean. Wind and rain slowly erode the exposed rock layers away. Eventually, the sandstone layer is revealed, and the fish fossil is ready to be found.

Background image: The badlands of South Dakota, where many fossils can be found.

A fish fossilizes slowly over time. Paleontologists dig carefully around exposed fossils so that they do not damage any parts that are still buried.

The Rarity of Fossils

It is actually quite unusual for an organism to turn into a fossil. Nature has a way of recycling life. Most dead organisms are eaten by animals. What doesn't get eaten is **decomposed**, that is, broken down by bacteria and oxygen into raw materials. Decomposed materials become part of the soil or the water and nourish new plants, helping them to grow.

Decomposition does not take very long. It has to work fast. Plants and animals die all the time. If they did not break down quickly, Earth would be covered with dead bodies!

If this bird does not become another animal's meal, bacteria will soon decompose its body.

Hard tissues such as teeth, bones, shells, and wood take longer to decompose than softer tissues such as skin or leaves. Hard parts of organisms have the best chance of being preserved as fossils.

Mineralization takes a long, long time. The remains or traces of a body usually need to be buried and undisturbed for thousands of years to turn to stone. But organisms can be

A mold fossil

Hard teeth and jawbones are often preserved as fossils after the skin and muscles of the animal decompose.

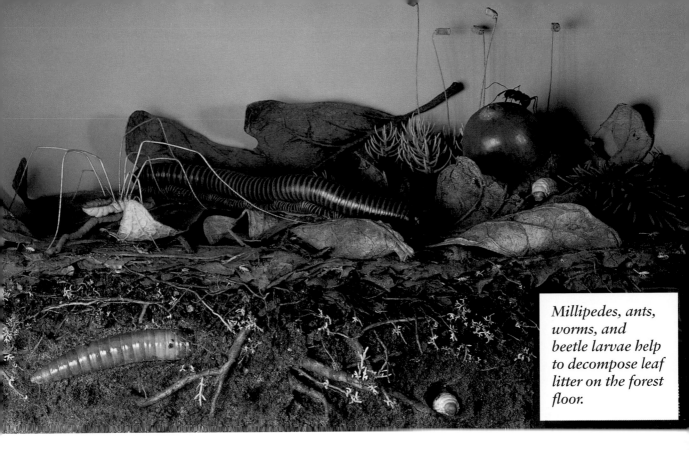

preserved in other ways as well.

Have you ever stepped in mud? You can see the tread from your shoe or, if you are barefoot, the shape of your toes and heel. If the mud hardens before it is disturbed, the imprint of your foot will be preserved. Similarly, when sediment hardens around the traces or remains of an organism, its outer shape and texture can be preserved as an imprint. Over time the mud hardens into rock. If the original object is removed, this imprint is called a **mold fossil**. Mold fossils often fill in with new sediment or other material. When this material hardens, it becomes a **cast fossil**, a rock with the exact surface shape of the original organism. Mold and cast fossils are often found together.

A cast fossil

You can see how this mold fossil (left) and cast fossil (right) fit together. Both preserve the surface shape of the original shell.

Remarkable Fossil Finds

How do we know that mammoths were "woolly"? Or that ancient insects had delicate wings? Or what the skin of ancient dinosaurs or the leaves from ancient ferns looked like? Sometimes, living things have been trapped in special material that preserves even the tiny details of their soft body parts.

People have found ancient insects preserved in hardened tree sap, called **amber**. Imagine a fly landing on a tree. It crawls across the rough bark, and gets stuck in something gooey. More tree sap oozes out of the bark and covers the insect entirely. Over time, the sap hardens and changes into amber, a clear yellow or orange substance, containing a perfectly preserved fly.

Mold fossils of ferns often preserve the intricate details of their leaves.

This unusual fossil (above) shows the dinosaur Oviraptor protecting its nest of eggs (as illustrated in the sketch, left).

Paleontologists also found a fossil of an Oviraptor egg which had cracked open, showing the bones of the developing animal.

Even the delicate antennae and legs of a praying mantis and its meal of ants have been preserved in this piece of amber.

A baby mammoth, which scientists named Dima, was found in Alaska almost perfectly preserved in permafrost (ground that never thaws).

Large mudslides and volcanic eruptions can bury many organisms at once. Entire forests of trees have been found fossilized in layers of volcanic ash. As with the fish bones in the sandstone, minerals were deposited in the wood of the trees, slowly turning it to stone. Fossilized wood is called **petrified wood**. Petrified means "turned to stone."

In Alaska, a bulldozer operator once dug up a frozen baby **mammoth**. Scientists think it might have lost its mother in a storm and fallen into a crevasse, a deep crack in the ice. Layers of snow, ice, and debris quickly buried it. Some places in Alaska are so cold that the ground beneath the surface never thaws. The baby mammoth stayed frozen for thousands of years. When it was found, its skin, hair, and even the last meal in its stomach were preserved. Just as the food you store in the freezer stays fresh, the body of a frozen animal does not decompose.

Petrified wood looks like real wood, but it is composed entirely of stony minerals.

Background image: Fossil dinosaur skin.

15

Who Studies Fossils?

Paleontology is the study of ancient life through fossils. Each individual fossil gives just a small clue about that life. Like detectives, paleontologists piece together many of these clues to learn how a particular organism looked and lived. Take the great dinosaurs, for example. Fossil bones suggest their size and shape. Fossil footprints suggest how heavy they were and how they moved. Fossilized dung and stomach contents show what they ate.

Paleontologists learn from **biologists,** who study the organisms living today. They compare modern organisms to what is known about fossil organisms.

Paleontologist Walter Granger was a great dinosaur hunter. He found and named many famous dinosaur fossils.

What biologists learn about the animals living today can be applied to the study of ancient life.

This helps them figure out how an ancient animal might have behaved, or what conditions were needed for certain plants to grow. Both biologists and paleontologists study how ancient organisms are related, and how they evolved into the organisms living today.

Geologists study the history of Earth through rocks. They learn how Earth's structure and climate have changed through its history. By learning about the rocks in which fossils are found, paleontologists can determine the environment in which those organisms lived. For example, sedimentary rock

Sedimentary rock layers, like those exposed in the badlands of South Dakota, are good places to find fossils of sea creatures.

reveals an environment where sediment settled out of water (a seafloor or riverbed), or where sediment was deposited by wind (a desert). Fossils found in volcanic rock made of ash

Ash from erupting volcanoes can bury and preserve organisms as it hardens into volcanic rock. Lava usually destroys any organism it touches.

Geologist George Billingsly uses a magnifying glass to study rocks more closely.

reveal organisms that lived where a volcano erupted.

You could say that paleontologists are both biologists and geologists. They work very hard, but many pieces in the story of life will never be found. Most organisms were never preserved. Still, Earth continues to surprise paleontologists as they uncover new fossils with more clues to its past. The ever-growing list of fossils that scientists use to understand Earth's history is called the **fossil record.**

"Reading" the Fossil Record

Imagine you could lay out all of Earth's fossils in front of you. The first thing you might notice is that many of the fossils look just like some of the plants and animals living today. Dragonflies, cockroaches, and horseshoe crabs are all "living fossils." The body plans of these animals have changed very little since their ancestors became fossils long ago. Somehow they survived as Earth went through many changes during its history.

Rock outcrops are good places to compare the kinds of fossils found in each layer of rock.

Organisms that could *not* survive the Earth's changes became **extinct** (died out). Most fossils represent plants and animals that no longer exist today.

Scientists have different ideas as to why these organisms went extinct. Perhaps their food source was no longer available, or they could not adapt to a change in climate.

Most fossils are found in layers of rock. Each individual layer is like a snapshot of the life on Earth at a particular time and in a particular environment. The fossils record the organisms that lived together, and the rock layer records the environment they lived in.

People thought an ancient fish called the coelacanth was extinct until fishermen caught one near South Africa in 1938. Coelacanths are among the oldest kinds of fish living today.

Modern dragonflies (left) have bodies very similar to those of fossils of their ancient ancestors (right).

We know that some kinds of organisms existed over a long time period because we find their fossils in many layers of rock. When fossils are found in only one or two layers of rock, scientists think those kinds of organisms did not exist on Earth for very long.

Scientists learn the relative age of fossils by looking at outcrops, places where you can see many rock layers all at once, like a layer cake. Because rock layers usually form on top of one other, newer layers usually lie above the older layers. That means a fossil in one layer is almost always younger than the fossils below it and older than the fossils on top of it. Paleontologists have to be careful, however. Sometimes, rock layers become folded and turned upside down as they are pushed up out of the ground.

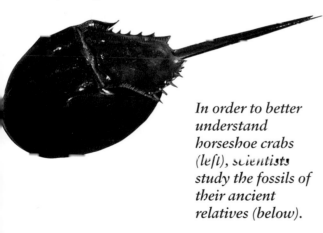

In order to better understand horseshoe crabs (left), scientists study the fossils of their ancient relatives (below).

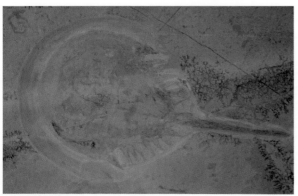

Sailors once told tales of the Dodo. This bird became extinct in the late 1600s, due mostly to over-hunting and the destruction of its nests by other animals.

Dynamic Earth

The ground you walk on seems solid and still. It isn't. Ever so slowly, it is moving. Earthquakes are quick, violent shifts of land, but usually you don't notice the constant shifting and changing of Earth's surface. Continents move toward each other, join, and break apart, but it happens over long periods of time. When continents collide, the seafloor, sediments, and fossils between them can be pushed up into mountains.

fossil fish

Fossils of tropical fish and ferns have been found in many places, including areas with cold climates.

fossil fern

The sea level slowly rises and falls as a result of Earth's changing surface. Unlike daily tides, causing the ocean to creep up and down the beach, worldwide sea level changes can be significant and long lasting. At times during Earth's history, oceans rose high enough to flood large areas of land. The flooded land became shallow oceans that remained for long stretches of time. When the sea level dropped again, layers of ocean sediment full of fossils were left behind on dry land. Today, people discover many fossils of sea creatures in the middle of continents far from any ocean.

This fossil coral (left) was found in the Grand Canyon— more than 500 miles from today's nearest ocean.

Earth's climate has also changed many times throughout its history. Different regions of Earth have gone from warm and wet to hot and dry, then to cold and icy, and back again. Scientists have found fossils of tropical plants near the South Pole. How could such plants have grown in the frigid temperatures and blizzards of Antarctica? They didn't. When those plants were alive, the land that is Antarctica today was a tropical paradise located near the equator!

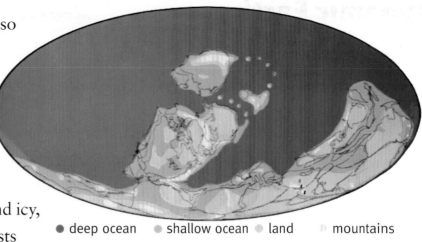

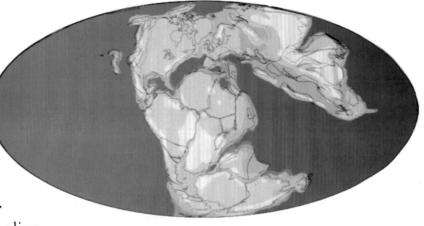

● deep ocean   ● shallow ocean   ● land   ● mountains

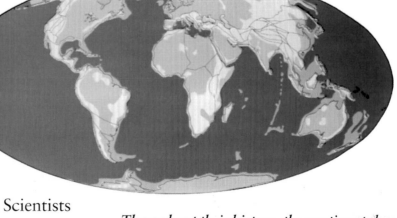

Certain parts of the fossil record show periods of time when many organisms became extinct all at once. Scientists think some of these mass extinctions may have been caused by the dynamic and ever-changing conditions on Earth.

Throughout their history, the continents have slowly moved around on Earth's surface. At one time most of the continents were in the southern hemisphere (top). Then they came together as one supercontinent called Pangaea (middle). Eventually they moved to their positions today (bottom). They are still moving.

Dynamic Life

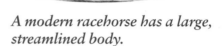

The fossil record reveals that life on Earth has changed over time. Most of the fossils found in older layers of rock are unlike the species (types of organisms) we are familiar with today. But many fossils in younger layers appear more similar to living species. What happened to the old species? How did the new species form?

Scientists think that species slowly changed throughout history as conditions changed on Earth. Over long periods of time, and many generations, organisms changed so much that they developed into completely new species. The species

A modern racehorse has a large, streamlined body.

that were best adapted to the changes in the environment survived and passed their characteristics to the next generation. This process is what scientists call evolution as explained by Charles Darwin. For example, the birds with beaks best adapted to feed on available food survived and passed their characteristics on to their offspring; cacti have survived because they have a

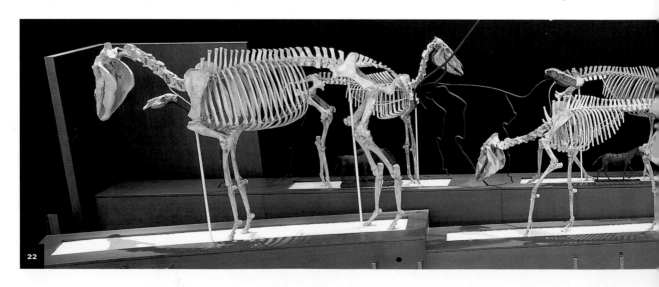

A small horse, the Shetland pony, is found in Scotland.

thick, waxy coating that helps them retain water in the dry desert.

Species can evolve in different ways if individuals from that species live in different conditions. One example is the case of okapis and giraffes. Okapis and giraffes are descended from a common ancestor and are both in the giraffe Family. The giraffe lives on open plains where the leaves it eats grow on tall trees. Over many generations the animals with longer necks survived and multiplied, passing their long necks and the potential to grow longer necks to their offspring.

The giraffe's close relative, the okapi, lives in jungles. The food it eats is far easier to reach, so an extremely long neck was not necessary for survival. Thus okapis do not share that characteristic with their close relative, the giraffe.

This museum exhibit illustrates how ideas about evolution have changed. Until recently evolution was viewed as a slow and steady progression, as shown in the front row of fossils. The row starts with the horse's ancestor, Hyracotherium *(far right), and shows a gradual progression of larger horse ancestors with fewer toes, better for carry the animal's larger body, and bigger teeth, better for eating tougher leaves and grasses. At the far left is* Equus, *very closely related to the modern horse. The back row shows many different horses that evolved from* Hyracotherium. *Some of its early descendants were large, and some of the later descendants smaller. These animals were successful for a time then died out. This exhibit shows that evolution is a not a straight road to bigger and better, but a road with a series of branches many of which come to dead ends.*

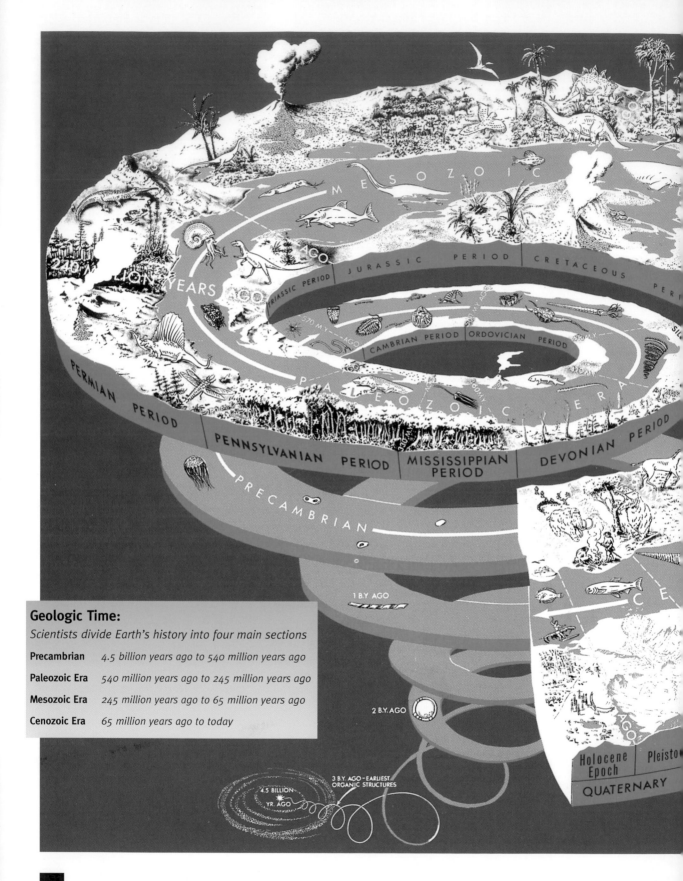

Geologic Time:

Scientists divide Earth's history into four main sections

Precambrian	*4.5 billion years ago to 540 million years ago*
Paleozoic Era	*540 million years ago to 245 million years ago*
Mesozoic Era	*245 million years ago to 65 million years ago*
Cenozoic Era	*65 million years ago to today*

The History of Life

The history of life is an epic story full of extraordinary creatures and dramatic events. The fossil record inspires scientists and artists alike to imagine and recreate extinct animals and environments in diagrams, drawings, and even in the movies.

Scientists at the US Geological Survey created this geologic time spiral to illustrate their understanding of how Earth has changed and evolved. Follow the spiral beginning at the bottom left, where it is thin and curly and says 4.5 BILLION YR. AGO (4.5 billion years ago). That is when many scientists think Earth formed. Proceed along the spiral to travel through time. As it gets wider and wider, you begin to see what organisms lived on Earth at different times according to the fossil record. Life as we know it today is shown at the widest end of the spiral.

The second half of this book introduces the history of life according to the evidence gathered by scientists. The story is complex and continues to change as new fossils and other clues are discovered. Use this time spiral as a reference while you learn about each era in Earth's history.

Geologic Time

It can be hard to understand just how old Earth is. Think of the oldest people you know. How old are they? 70? 80? 100 years old? For humans, they have lived long lives, but compared to the estimated age of the Earth, they are just babies. 100 years compared to 4.5 billion years (4,500,000,000 years) is like comparing the number of sand grains you can stick to your fingertip to an entire beach full of sand.

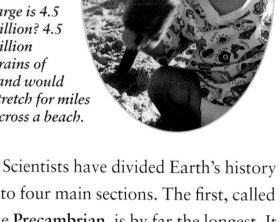

Just how large is 4.5 billion? 4.5 billion grains of sand would stretch for miles across a beach.

Scientists have divided Earth's history into four main sections. The first, called the **Precambrian,** is by far the longest. It begins with the formation of Earth and ends when many of the first simple life forms went extinct.

Earth is extremely old.

The three following sections are called eras. They have nicknames based on the kinds of life that dominated Earth at that time. The **Paleozoic Era** (meaning "ancient life") is sometimes known as the Age of Trilobites. The **Mesozoic Era** (meaning "middle life") is often called the Age of Dinosaurs. The **Cenozoic Era** (meaning "recent life") is the era we are currently living in. It is sometimes called the Age of Mammals, but it could just as easily be called the Age of Birds or the Age of Insects.

To get an idea of how long each section lasts, imagine that Earth's history could be compressed into one day—24 hours. The Precambrian would last from midnight until about 7:30 in the evening (19:30 PM)! The Paleozoic Era would last about two and a half hours until 10:00 PM (22:00 PM).

The Mesozoic Era would last a little over an hour— up to 11:15 PM (23:15 PM). Finally, the Cenozoic Era would last just forty-five minutes. Life as we know it today would squeeze into the last second of the day: 11:59 PM and 59 seconds (23:59 PM).

Scientists further divide the four geologic sections into **periods**. The names of many periods refer to the location where the first fossils from that period were found.

This clock is divided into 24 hours, instead of the usual 12. The black line indicates the relative length of the Precambrian compared with the three other eras (indicated in green).

Cenozoic Era (Age of Recent Life)	Quaternary Period	The several geologic eras were originally named Primary, Secondary, Tertiary, Quaternary. The first two names are no longer used. Tertiary and Quaternary have been retained but used as period designations.
	Tertiary Period	
Mesozoic Era (Age of Middle Life)	Cretaceous Period	Derived from the Latin word for chalk (creta) and first applied to extensive deposits that form white cliffs along the English Channel.
	Jurassic Period	Named for the Jura Mountains, located between France and Switzerland, where rocks of this age were first studied.
	Triassic Period	Taken from the word "trias" in recognition of the threefold character of these rocks in Europe.
Paleozoic Era (Age of Ancient Life)	Permian Period	Named after the province of Perm, in the former Soviet Union, where these rocks were first studied.
	Pennsylvanian Period	Named for the State of Pennsylvania where these rocks have produced much coal.
	Mississippian Period	Named for the Mississippi River valley where these rocks are well exposed.
	Devonian Period	Named after Devonshire, England where these rocks were first studied.
	Silurian Period	Named after Celtic tribes, the Silures and the Ordovices, that lived in Wales during the Roman Conquest.
	Ordovician Period	
	Cambrian Period	Taken from the Roman name for Wales (Cambria) where rocks containing the earliest evidence of complex forms of life were first studied.
Precambrian	– – – – – – –	The time between the birth of the planet and the appearance of complex forms of life. More than 80 percent of the Earth's estimated 4 1/2 billion years falls within this era.

This table shows the periods within each era and describes the origins of each name.

The Precambrian

According to scientists, Earth began as a ball of gases and fiery bursts of hot lava. There was no ground to walk on and the sky was black both day and night. Meteorites bombarded Earth, creating huge craters. You could not have lived back then because there was no oxygen to breathe. It took millions of years for Earth to begin to settle down and harden. More than one fifth (1/5) of Earth's entire history passed before any life at all existed.

Eventually, warm water covered Earth like a hot, thick chemical soup. These chemicals were the ingredients of life. Tiny, simple organisms formed from them. They weren't plants or animals but a kind of bacteria called **cyanobacteria**. They thrived in the tropical seas, and some grew into large colonies, called **stromatolites**, that resembled coral reefs. They also began to fill the water and the air with oxygen, and as a result, the daytime sky turned blue.

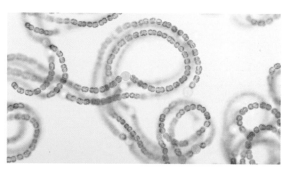

Cyanobacteria, some of Earth's earliest life forms (above), still grow today in colonies called stromatolites (below).

Lava bubbles out of the Paricutin Volcano, Mexico.

Slowly, these bacteria started to change shape and size to form more complex organisms. Over time the oceans became full of jellyfish-like creatures with long tentacles floating past wormlike creatures slithering over the sandy bottom.

Many ancient organisms had soft bodies. Some may have looked like these modern slime molds.

Other soft-bodied animals with tiny legs crawled over stromatolites and sponge-like organisms that grew out of the seafloor.

Volcanic eruptions and earthquakes shook Earth even as life evolved in its oceans. Lava hardened and built up rocky islands rising out of the water. Over time, Earth's temperature cooled. Perhaps ash from the volcanoes filled the sky blocking the sun. Many of the creatures could not survive in the colder water. All but a few became extinct.

Dust and ash from a volcano fills the air and darkens the sky. This may be what the sky of early Earth looked like.

29

Precambrian Evidence

Many meteorites, such as the Willamette found in Oregon, reveal information about the formation of Earth.

More than seven eighths (7/8) of Earth's history occurred during the Precambrian. The fossil record does not provide much evidence for this time, because almost all of the earliest organisms were tiny and had no easily preserved hard parts. Of the few fossils that formed, most have eroded away or been buried deep in the ground. Instead, scientists look at rocks to learn about Earth's beginnings.

Bacteria living today near black smokers at the bottom of the oceans are similar to some of the earliest forms of life.

Scientists use complex methods to learn the age of rocks. They have uncovered many ancient rocks thought to be some of the earliest to form on Earth. They have also found **meteorites**, rocky objects from space that crashed into Earth. Evidence suggests that many of these meteorites crashed onto Earth as it was forming. Small meteorites still crash on Earth today, but much less often than they did early in the planet's history.

The earliest known fossils are of cyanobacteria. They may look like very simple organisms, but don't let that fool you. They were the dominant life form in the fossil record for almost half Earth's history. Cyanobacteria released oxygen gas into the water and air. This

oxygen helped to create Earth's atmosphere with its blue skies. They are some of the most important bacteria on Earth and exist even today. Their bodies produce a cementlike material that combines with sediment to create great reeflike structures called stromatolites. In some oceans, stromatolites are still found today.

Very few fossils of other Precambrian organisms had been found until a geologist discovered some rocks in the Ediacara Hills of Australia. They contained fossils of soft-bodied animals, including imprints of creatures that look a lot like worms and jellyfish. Scientists think they are some of the first good evidence of complex life.

Cyanobacteria still thrive and create stromatolites, like these in Australia.

The Paleozoic Era

At the beginning of the Paleozoic Era, there was an explosion of life. New creatures floated, swam, crawled, and slithered in the tropical seas. Sponges busily built vast new reefs. Trilobites with their segmented bodies and many legs scavenged on the seafloor. Small fish swam with their mouths open, filtering tiny plankton from the water. A new group of fish developed bones— the first *bony* fish. With their sharp teeth and huge jaws, they looked quite ferocious. Creatures which had developed elaborate shells, armor, and sharp spines were able to protect their soft bodies from these eager predators.

Large masses of land, called continents, moved slowly across Earth's surface. Waves lapped on rocky beaches, and the warm sun encouraged thick mats of algae and small plants to grow on the shore. As the plants developed stems and roots to support their bodies, they grew taller and could live farther from the water.

A diorama of an ancient seafloor shows rugose coral and trilobites.

This artist's illustration shows aquatic life thriving in a Paleozoic bay.

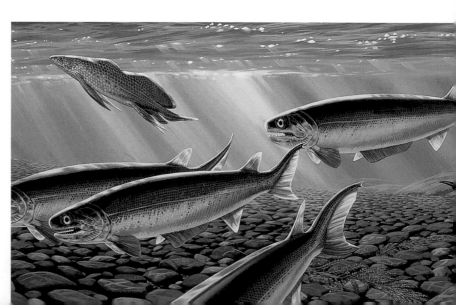

This artist's illustration of Paleozoic life includes early fish and amphibians, some venturing onto land.

Creatures began to leave the water to feed on ferns, trees, and other plants covering the coastlines. Worms burrowed in the soil. Insects developed wings and began to fly. Fishlike creatures waddled up on shore on primitive legs to feed but returned to the water to reproduce, as modern amphibians still do today. Some developed tough, dry, reptilian skin, and spent more and more time out of the water. They began laying their eggs on land.

The different landmasses where these creatures lived slowly moved toward one another. Eventually they all joined together into one huge supercontinent called **Pangaea**. Mountains formed, the climate became drier, the sea saltier, and the greatest mass extinction in history occurred. Almost all the marine animals, most amphibians, and many kinds of reptiles and plants died out. This marked the end of the Paleozoic Era.

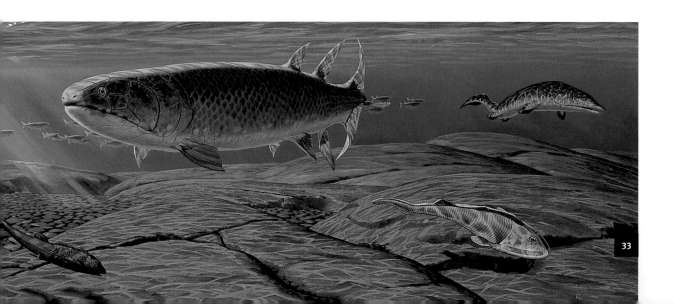

Paleozoic Evidence

Possibly the best known animal from the Paleozoic Era is the **trilobite**, a segmented animal that lived in the ocean. Scientists have found more than 15,000 kinds of trilobites— some no bigger than a pencil's eraser, others more than two feet long. Some crawled on the seafloor, others burrowed in the sand, and still more learned to swim. Trilobite means "three lobes." Each had a hard outer covering with three lobes, or humps, running down its back. After thriving in the oceans during this era, they became extinct. No one understands exactly why.

The Burgess Shale in the Canadian Rocky Mountains has well-preserved fossils from the Paleozoic Era.

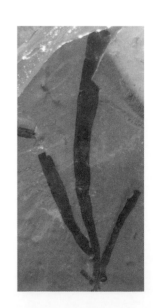

In a remote and protected region in the mountains of western Canada, there are many trilobite remains: a fossil hunter's paradise. A rock formation called the Burgess Shale was formed from mudflows at the beginning of the Paleozoic Era. Thick layers of mud buried thousands of sea animals and even preserved some of the first kinds of plants. Here scientists have found not only the skeletons of trilobites but also imprints of algae and even the gut contents of some worms.

A trilobite fossil found in the Burgess Shale, Canada.

A fossil sponge from the Burgess Shale.

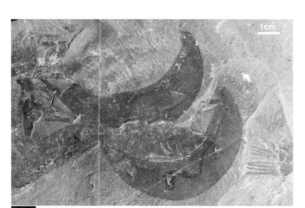

Fossil worms from the Burgess Shale.

At the Grand Canyon in Arizona, you can see almost the entire Paleozoic Era laid out before you. Over thousands of years, the Colorado River cut a canyon a mile deep through the many layers of sedimentary rock that formed during the Paleozoic Era. From a distance, the layers look like stripes on the canyon wall. Up close you can see fossils in each layer. From the uppermost rim down to the canyon floor, the Grand Canyon is a magnificent outcrop known as much for its beauty as for its fossil record.

The Grand Canyon in Arizona is a beautiful place where rock layers from almost the entire Paleozoic Era can be seen all at once.

Brachiopod fossils are often found in mudstone, a sedimentary rock. Brachiopods were among the first animals to develop shells around their bodies.

The Mesozoic Era

New and more complex organisms populated the oceans. Oysters and clams burrowed in sand and clung to rocky shores. Spiny sea urchins and small bony fish took up residence in coral reefs. Squidlike creatures hid from the sharp teeth of sharks and other large fish. The fiercest predators, however, were the marine reptiles. With huge, streamlined bodies and strong flippers, **ichthyosaurs** and **mosasaurs** could outswim almost any prey.

On land, the deserts were hot and dry. Most plants hugged the coasts, forming tropical forests and swamps.

This model of velociraptor reconstructs how scientists think these dinosaurs looked.

The sky was abuzz with flying insects, and the ground was alive with crawling creatures. Frogs, salamanders, and turtles had plenty to eat. Quick, crocodilelike animals learned to run on their powerful hind legs. Over time, enormous **dinosaurs** arose, the largest land animals during this era.

An artist's illustration of Mesozoic life shows a flying Pterosaur *in the air and a large marine reptile hunting fish in the sea.*

An artist's illustration of Mesozoic life in the desert includes velociraptors *chasing* Protoceratops *and an* Oviraptor *standing by its nest of eggs.*

Pangaea slowly broke apart into many continents separated by shallow seas, thus isolating organisms on each continent. More rain began to fall. Large forests and open woodlands developed and the deserts shrank. The forests and swamps bloomed with the flowering plants that were evolving.

An artist's illustration of Mesozoic life in swamps and forests depicts a fierce dinosaur battle.

A few smaller land animals developed hair, had live babies instead of laying eggs, and became the first mammals. They scurried around on the ground and hid from the dinosaurs. Some dinosaurs made attempts to fly. Over many generations, these animals developed lighter bones and stronger muscles for flapping their arms. Eventually they became the first birds.

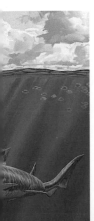

Life was thriving, but another mass extinction occurred. Was it because of a change in climate? Did a large meteorite hit the Earth? No one knows why, but most of the dinosaurs, the large marine predators, and many other plants and animals became extinct. This extinction marked the end of the Mesozoic Era.

Mesozoic Evidence

Mary Anning, known as the "greatest fossilist the world ever knew," grew up on the coast of England in the early 1800's. As a child, she loved to help her father find fossils on the local beaches to sell in his cabinet-making shop. When still a young girl, she discovered the first complete fossil of an ichthyosaur, an ancient marine reptile with sharp teeth and a dolphinlike body.

Around the same time in England, Sir Richard Owen named a group of new fossils whose bones were larger than any living land animal. Despite their size, the bones looked similar to those of reptiles. So he called them "terrible great lizards," or dinosaurs. A great number of paleontologists competed to discover and identify the most dinosaurs. Along the way, they also found fossils of early mammals and birds.

Ichthyosaur fossil reveals the animal's strong jaw, paddlelike legs, and long tail.

Later, she discovered another ocean predator from the Mesozoic Era, the long-necked **plesiosaur**. Mary did not have a formal science education. She taught herself to identify bones and became such an expert that scientists came from all over the world to consult with her.

Mary Anning found the first complete ichthyosaur fossil.

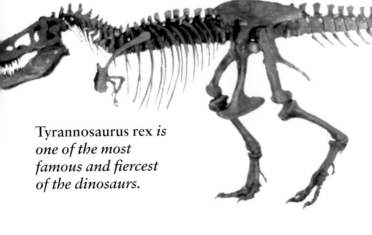

Tyrannosaurus rex is one of the most famous and fiercest of the dinosaurs.

Sir Richard Owen (right) coined the name "dinosaur" to describe the huge, reptilelike fossils from the Mesozoic Era.

Another naturalist, Roy Chapman Andrews, grew up dreaming of adventure. He worked his way up from scrubbing floors at the American Museum of Natural History to become one of its most famous paleontologists. In the 1920s, he led fossil-hunting expeditions to the Gobi Desert in Mongolia. Amid sandstorms, snakes, and bandits, his team discovered an incredible site for dinosaur fossils. Dinosaur eggs, nests, and skeletons from the Gobi Desert have revealed important evidence showing that dinosaurs were the ancestors to birds.

Roy Chapman Andrews (above) discovered many dinosaur fossils in the Gobi Desert of Mongolia.

Birdlike **Oviraptor**, plant-eating **Protoceratops**, and the quick, vicious **Velociraptor** all were first identified in the Gobi Desert.

The Cenozoic Era

The continents began to move very slowly toward their current locations. Ice formed at the north and south poles. Sea levels dropped and more land was exposed. Tropical forests and swampy environments still existed near the equator, but the temperature cooled near the icy poles. Scientists think that organisms evolved separately on each continent, creating a great variety of life. Mammals, birds, and insects of all shapes and sizes began to thrive. Great cats stalked the large herds of hoofed mammals that grazed on wide-open grasslands. Monkeys gorged themselves on the fruit from trees and bushes.

An artist's illustration of Cenozoic life along a river includes early snakes, crocodiles, turtles, and fish.

Hummingbirds flitted from flower to flower drinking nectar.

Scientists think that some mammals returned to the sea and evolved into whales. Octopuses hid among schools of brightly colored fish, while large sharks and rays  patrolled the water looking for a meal. Large turtles basked on sunny logs, and crocodiles lurked just beneath the water.

An artist's illustration of Cenozoic life in grasslands shows early versions of horses, elephants, and rhinoceroses, among other animals.

An artist's illustration of life in a Cenozoic valley depicts wolf and catlike predators stalking large mammals.

Early humans began to make tools, harvest plants, use fire for cooking, and make cave drawings. They migrated to all parts of the world.

Later in the Cenozoic Era, the temperature dropped worldwide, and more ice formed at the poles. Organisms adapted to the colder environments, moved to warmer regions, or became extinct. Large mammals developed thick fur and layers of fat to stay warm. Some animals learned to slow down their bodies and hibernate. For a few thousand years, organisms had to crowd into the few areas where ice had not formed or else they went extinct.

The ice eventually melted as Earth's climate warmed again. Some ice-age organisms may not have adapted and became extinct. Others survived and returned to places previously covered in ice. Humans settled down to live in communities.

Cenozoic Evidence

Fossils from the Cenozoic Era show how diverse life has become. Fossils in Australia, North America, and Africa represent quite different organisms.

One of the most famous fossil sites for Cenozoic life sits in the middle of Los Angeles. It is called La Brea Tar Pits and tells the story of southern California long before there were cities.

Plants flourished near shallow pools of water. Animals came to find shade and get a drink. Little did they know that beneath some of these pools **asphalt** bubbled up out of the ground. Asphalt, also known as tar, is very sticky. Many unsuspecting animals got stuck in the asphalt. Predators and scavengers heard their cries of distress and hurried to the pools to get an easy meal. They too became stuck. As asphalt continued to seep from the ground, it buried the animals all together in a great, big, sticky graveyard.

Fossils of giant mammals such as the woolly mammoths, mastodons, bison, giant ground sloths, and saber-toothed cats have been found at La Brea Tar Pits.

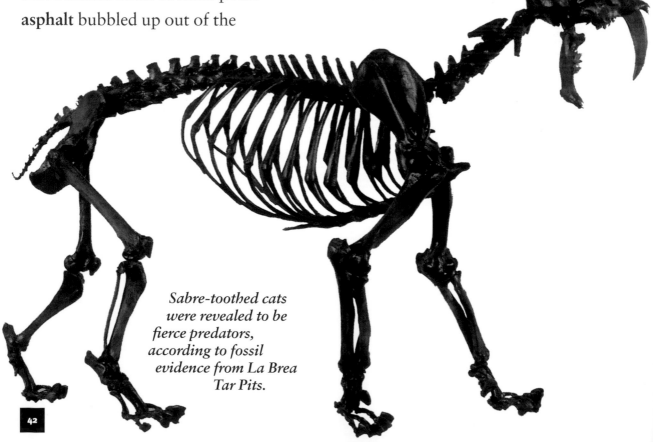

Sabre-toothed cats were revealed to be fierce predators, according to fossil evidence from La Brea Tar Pits.

An artist's illustration of La Brea Tar Pits late in the Cenozoic Era suggests how scientists think animals became stuck in the asphalt.

Trees from ancient forests were also buried there, along with rodents, birds, and smaller mammals. Even a human has been uncovered!

Asphalt still seeps out of the ground there today, so uncovering the fossils is slow, dirty work. But it is worth the trouble. La Brea fossils are almost perfectly preserved by the asphalt, and they have helped scientists learn many details about the plants, animals, and climate of the Cenozoic Era.

In addition to the one from La Brea, early human fossils continue to be discovered all over the world. They reveal how our ancestors lived, which gives us a greater understanding of ourselves today.

To this day animals still become trapped in the asphalt at La Brea Tar Pits.

The Fascination with Fossils

Long ago, when fossils such as this ancient shark jaw were found, people could only imagine the kind of creatures they might have belonged to.

A fossil is shown here used as a necktie.

Fossils have fascinated people for thousands of years. Long before we knew much about the giant dinosaurs, mammoths, and marine predators, their bones inspired stories of dragons, giant ogres, and sea monsters.

Fossils have also been very useful to humans. Evidence shows that early humans probably used sharp teeth from animals as tools and weapons. In the thousands of years since then, the teeth have become fossils. Fossil were used as jewelry and people buried them with their dead. They are still used in making jewelry and other objects today.

Oil refineries process and refine crude oil, a fossil fuel, for everything from gasoline to plastic bags.

Today, many of our most important energy resources come from fossils. We burn coal, made from fossil plants, and oil, made from tiny fossil organisms, to give us heat and energy. Coal and oil are two kinds of **fossil fuels.**

Perhaps most important of all is the role fossils play in reconstructing Earth's past. The fossil record helps us understand life and its presence on Earth. From the first tiny bacteria to the most complex plants and animals, Earth has hosted an amazing variety of organisms throughout its history.

The proof is in the fossils.

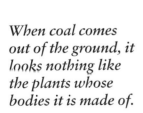

When coal comes out of the ground, it looks nothing like the plants whose bodies it is made of.

Using wire, scientists reconstructed the front half of this partial Mesozoic fish fossil.

Glossary

amber A hard yellowish substance formed from fossilized tree sap.

asphalt A black, tar-like substance.

biologist A scientist who studies living things.

cast fossil A rock that hardens inside a mold fossil (see mold fossil).

Cenozoic Era The most recent era of geologic time in Earth's history. The Cenozoic Era lasted from about 65 million years ago through today.

continent A great landmass on the surface of the Earth.

cyanobacteria A tiny bacteria that was one of the first forms of life on Earth.

decompose To rot or decay.

decomposition The process by which organic materials rot or decay.

dinosaur Animals characterized by a hole in their hip socket. Giant dinosaurs thrived in the Mesozoic Era. Modern birds are the descendents of the Mesozoic dinosaurs.

Equus The genus name scientists give to the group of animals that includes the modern horse.

evolution The gradual change of organisms over many generations creating new species.

extinct No longer existing. If a certain type of organism is extinct, it means all individuals of that type have died out.

fossil Any evidence of an ancient organism preserved over time in rock.

fossil fuel A fuel made from compressed (squashed) bodies of organisms that died long ago. Coal, oil, and gas are all fossil fuels.

fossil record The ever-growing list of fossils that scientists study in order to understand Earth's history.

geologist A scientist who studies Earth's soil and rocks.

Hyracotherium An ancestral relative of modern horses.

Ichthyosaur An type of extinct marine reptile that lived in the Mesozoic Era. Ichthyosaurs had dolphin-shaped bodies and narrow, tooth-filled "beaks."

mammoth An ancient elephantlike animal with long, curving tusks. Some had shaggy hair. Mammoths lived during the ice age.

Mesozoic Era The period of geologic time during which the great dinosaurs lived. The Mesozoic Era lasted from about 245 million years ago until about 65 million years ago.

meteorite A rocky object in space that falls to earth.

mineral A nonliving substance found in the earth. Most rocks are made of minerals.

mineralization The process by which minerals harden to form rock.

mold fossil An imprint made by an organism that has been preserved in rock.

Mosasaur An type of extinct giant marine lizard that lived in the Mesozoic Era. Mosasaurs had long heads, large jaws, strong and flexible necks, and two pairs of paddles for legs.

organism A living thing.

Oviraptor A small, bird-like dinosaur that moved quickly on its two long legs. *Oviraptor* had a long tail, a curved neck, powerful jaws, and a strong beak.

paleontologist A scientist who studies prehistoric life.

Paleozoic Era The period of geologic time known as "ancient life." The Paleozoic Era lasted from about 540 million years ago until about 245 million years ago.

Pangaea The name scientists give to the sole huge continent that once existed on Earth. Pangaea gradually split apart to form the seven continents we have today.

period In geologic time, a subsection of each geologic era.

petrified wood Wood that has turned into stone because minerals have seeped into its cells and hardened.

Plesiosaur A type of extinct marine reptile that lived in the Mesozoic Era. Plesiosaurs had large bodies with narrow heads, long necks, and two pairs of paddles.

Precambrian The first and longest section of geologic time. The Precambrian began about 4.5 billion years ago and lasted until many of the first simple life forms went extinct about 540 million years ago.

Protoceratops A relatively slow dinosaur that ate plants and walked on four short legs.

sedimentary rock Rock formed from sediment (such as particles of sand, soil, and mud).

species A group of organisms that share many characteristics. Members of the same species can mate and produce more organisms like themselves.

stromatolite A large colony of cynobacteria that grows like a reef in the ocean.

trace fossil The preserved mark of an animal that lived long ago. Footprints and toothmarks in rock are examples of trace fossils.

trilobite An extinct animal that lived in Paleozoic seas. Trilobites had many legs, oval-shaped bodies divided into three lobes, and were ancestors to insects.

Velociraptor A fast, two-legged meat-eating dinosaur with about 80 sharp teeth and long, retractable claws on the middle toe of each foot.

Index